TABLE OF CONTENTS

PREFACE

When I sat down to begin writing *The Petals Fall One by One* at the beginning of quarantine in March of 2020, I had no intention of writing a book. I was a third-year college student at Chapman University, studying Kinesiology. Ironic, I know. Although, dating back to high school, I wrote poems to express my feelings, but I never shared them. I took a temporary hiatus when I transitioned into college; however, by the time quarantine rolled around, I was enrolled in a creative writing class, so I began writing more poetry during the worldwide lockdown. In the beginning, I wrote about themes and feelings I was experiencing in my life. As the months progressed, I realized that I had amassed over one hundred poems, and they all had an overarching theme: love, one of the deepest and most powerful emotions there is. At that point, I aimed my focus toward writing a book. I began to incorporate stories and experiences of loved ones, which added to the anecdotes that I had already written about my own life. Nine months later, here I am with the complete version of *The Petals Fall One by One*.

The Petals Fall One by One chronicles the rollercoaster of love, life, heartbreak, and new beginnings. It is based on authentic experiences, whether my own or a loved one's, and is meant to help you remember that everyone is human. We are all on this journey of life together, figuring ourselves and one another out, one day at a time.

A flower names each chapter in the book. Each flower has a different literary representation, and the poems within each chapter relate to the literary understanding of that specific flower:

1. The first chapter is entitled ROSES. Roses represent romance and passionate love. These poems describe what being in love feels like, including the good and the bad.

2. The second chapter is entitled PROTEAS, which represent change and transformation. In this chapter, poems discuss themes of realization while touching on different perspectives of life and our time on earth.

3. The third chapter is entitled DAFFODILS, which symbolize rebirth and new beginnings. The poems in this chapter surround themes of starting anew while reflecting on the past.

4. The fourth chapter is entitled ORCHIDS, which exemplify themes of refinement and maturity. In

this chapter, the poems consider hypotheticals that didn't work out while also touching on the themes of growth and wisdom.

5. The fifth and final chapter is entitled SWEET PEAS, and these flowers represent appreciation and departure. The poems in the final chapter consider themes of healing, longing, and yearning of what once was, but also remind you that after the dust settles and the storm clears, life goes on.

Overall, my motivation stemmed from quarantine and the Covid-19 pandemic. I wanted to find a way to connect with others on a mental and emotional basis, even while being in several different places. More importantly, most of my motivation originates from my grandparents, great-grandparents, and uncles, who have transitioned onto the next realm. Each of them saw so much potential in me, and I only hope that I continue to fulfill that potential, along with the plan that God has for my life.

Lastly, I am grateful for you and the journey we are about to embark on together. Thank you for reading and for giving me a chance.

December 2020

Acknowledgements

Writing a book is no easy feat. From writing upwards of 200 poems, condensing that list down to the final 100, then editing that list even further, I could not have done it alone. I want to thank two of my closest friends, Jordan Coleman-Stithz and David Robinson, for their keen insight and support from the start. I have been friends with Jordan for the last nine years and David for the last seven, and they have stood by me through thick and thin. Thank you both for your time, your dedication, and your excitement towards my book! Thank you both for answering my sporadic texts and random facetimes whenever I was unsure about the book's sequencing, and for the hours on end spent editing and ensuring that my best work shined through. Thank you both for giving honest advice and critique, but thank you even more for being great friends. *The Petals Fall One by One* would not have come to life without either of you.

A brief thank you to my Aunt Nicole Gray as well. Thanks for buying me that notebook. When I started writing the poems for my book, I wrote on pieces of loose-leaf paper and you bought me a notebook because you were tired of seeing the unorganized pages everywhere. You told me you had hopes of me doing something big when you gave the notebook to me, and I hope I'm making you proud.

To my parents: I would not have made it through this process without either of you. Thank you both for always believing in me and for the ongoing support through all of my life endeavors. Thank you, mom, for listening to me vent and reassuring me even when I have felt discouraged throughout this process, and thank you, dad, for pushing me to continue writing and to continue improving my writing skills. I love you both!

Finally, to everyone else who has been a cornerstone in my life along the way: Mama, Grammy, Chee Chee, Amya, Amari, Austin, Brooklynn, Alicia, Rodney, Uncle Dwain, Uncle G, Auntie Christina, Uncle Little, Kameron, Kristopher, Akilah, Lil' Dwain, Kai, and to all the rest of my aunts, uncles, cousins, family, and friends -- thank you.

LEGACY

Two losses in five days

Father, I know that you work in mysterious ways.

I try not to question,

And just accept your blessings,

But I don't have the capacity to understand

What is your final plan?

It doesn't make sense,

Here one day and gone the next.

I hurt for my grandmother who lost two brothers

I hurt for my great-grandmother who lost two sons,

Now they're resting alongside you up above, looking
down upon their loved ones.

Poppy, Granddaddy, Grandma, Pops, Uncle Charles,
Uncle Bobby:

May you all continue to look down and guide me,

May you all continue to be my angels that walk beside
me.

roses

romance and passion

ONE BY ONE

As a rose begins to blossom,
It begins to shed its layers
It begins to open up and give insight

Yet as it gets older,
The petals begin to fall one by one
And they lay where they fall
When everything is said and done.

Scattered across the floor like emotions,
I pick them up one at a time,
The petals lay where they fall
Welcome to our journey,
You're along for the ride.

UNCERTAIN

The push and pull
Results from the past
Trauma and mistakes stacked on top of each other from
years passed
I want this to be my last
Because,
I'm tired.

Tired of falling short, tired of being let down
Tired of pouring in and not getting the same support

So I'm hoping that you continue to see my soul
That you continue to peel back my layers to see my
transparency
I'm hoping that we continue to build,
And that we can push forward but never have to pull
back.

FOR YOU

You look at me,

And I get caught in your gaze.

Hazel eyes that open into the abyss,

We are one.

On the same network,

Intertwined, connected,

Our skin not needing to touch,

Because our souls are tied;

I hold you down, you ride for me

Just us, how I always imagined it to be.

THE LONG HAUL

Is this worth fighting for?

This thing that you and I have,

Is it worth fighting for?

I wonder if it's us or just me…

FRESH WOUNDS

Let's rewind the hands of time to when we first met
Two naive souls looking for love,
We were both healing.
Your wounds almost closed
And mine still fresh from months beforehand--
We gave it a try.

You revealed yourself deeper than surface
While I was too afraid to take off my band-aid
You opened up to me
And took me by surprise
Then you pushed me to be vulnerable too,
But it was all a guise.

You wanted to seem like the bigger person,
As if you were ready to love--
In all reality, you were never as pure as a dove;
The deceit was new and very unexpected of you
Yet I only knew you for a few months
What was a man to do?

I'LL DO BETTER NEXT TIME

Empty conversations

Resulting in nothing

Filling the air with meaningless words

You never hold your word

Wasting your breath

Trying to prove a point

You lost me at,

"I promise I'll do better this time."

Too many second chances,

You've become complacent.

Your words saying one thing

Your actions showing another,

You're stuck in your ways,

But I'm too attached to let you go.

COLOR BLIND

She saw the signs,
She still overextended
She saw the flags,
She gave him the benefit of the doubt

She needed to stop looking with her heart
And start realizing with her eyes
That regardless of his potential,
He'd never be able to fulfill it.

CAUGHT IN THE MIDDLE

In a space between I care

And you're a stranger.

PASSENGER

I noticed that you noticed me.

That you listen to hear me

That you seek to understand, with no ulterior plans.

It makes me uncomfortable,

Because nobody has ever listened to me before.

I usually listen and carry the conversation,

I usually listen and carry the relationship,

But

It's a nice change to not have to drive,

To be able to sit back and simply enjoy the ride.

JUST ENOUGH

Pieces of paper in the printer,
Is there enough to print what I need?

Will I need more,
Will I need less?

As the ink fills the pages, I'm waiting for the finished
product,
Not knowing if I will need to add more
Not knowing if there will be enough;

Similar to finding a new love--
Not knowing if I need to open up more
Or not knowing if I opened up enough;

But the printing is over,
We're now married,
And you were the perfect amount of paper I needed.

FOUR-LEAF CLOVER

Her essence and aura

Filled the room before she ever opened her mouth

She was of gold

One of a kind

I'm grateful to have her, I'm lucky she's mine.

ATMOSPHERE

My stomach is in knots,

Incapable of breathing

I'm gasping for air,

But you have all of the oxygen.

You're so distant, I can't reach you

Your love deep enough to reach the crypts of my
stomach,

I need you here;

So I can refill my lungs,

And breathe fresh air.

TUG OF WAR

She pushes

He pulls

One second she wants him

The next minute she doesn't

He is trying to win her back,

But she's tired.

Time is wasting away playing tug of war

He wants to right his wrongs,

When they should've been on the same team from the start.

FAKE LOVE

Do you really love me?

Or have the words been said for so long,

Through all that we've been through,

That they've become a default?

Rolling off the tip of your tongue like saliva

They become meaningless,

Then you go back to doing what you were doing.

No heart reflection,

No mental connection,

Because you have love for me,

But you no longer love me.

CHOOSE WISELY

Caught in between love and lust

Does she want me for me?

In her, can I confide my trust?

Or is it all for show

Because it's an hour past midnight,

And her ex just hit her phone.

Emotionally Unintelligent

Feelings invalidated
As if I don't exist
As if I am living in a fantasy
Or I'm crazy;

Not making sense, you belittle me
To uplift yourself,
Ultimately, you're insecure.

Projecting your vulnerabilities
Onto me, but not seeing the wrong
Is immature,
But you grew up guarded,
And sheltered;

Yet I can't blame you,
You're just a product of your environment.

POINT OF NO RETURN

It's gotten to the point
Where there's no return.
Where there are no lessons left to be learned,
And no tables left unturned,
It's too late.
Too blind to see my side,
To live a day in my shoes,
To comprehend my mind,
You're too self-sufficient.
Not in means of supporting yourself
But almost too self-righteous,
As if you were in a crisis, but think you had it all figured
out.

But to be honest, I don't mind
We're at the point of no return.

WOULD YOU

Would you call me if you needed me,

Or would you be too afraid to overstep?

Would you text me if you missed me,

Or would you be too guarded to show your heart?

Then I wonder:

The same things I do for you,

Would you do for me too?

I'D RATHER

I'd rather give more,

Than not give enough.

I'd rather shed my layers

To reveal my heart and let you in,

Than bluff.

I'd rather lay it all out on the table

Than leave you outside on the surface,

Questioning our purpose.

I share the stories, the experiences, and the memories that
make me,

With you,

Revealing parts of me that nobody has ever seen,

In hopes,

That you will too.

LIFELONG

It's been a while,

A lot has changed:

The fruits have grown,

But she is still the same.

Her authenticity never lost in the midst,

She stayed grounded and focused

Even in the thick of it all.

And for her I am grateful

And for her I am thankful.

proteas

realization, change, transformation

SUNRISE

The rooster crows as dawn is breaking

A new day has begun, another chance

A chance to be better than you were yesterday

But not perfect because there's still tomorrow

There's still your whole lifetime

Take it day by day, hour by hour

Be grateful you're still here,

Many would wish to be.

FOOTPRINT

Like a resounding gong,

Or a broken record,

History repeats itself.

Life keeps going,

But what will you pass on?

What will your footprint be?

12 A.M. THOUGHTS

Peace: A word so heavy but so light at once

What does it mean to be at peace?

Is it the ocean tide flowing in and out

Is it admiring the myriad of stars in the night sky,

Is it spending time with the one you love

Or could it be doing the thing you have a passion for?

Peace can be hard to come by

The worries of life clouding our views

The stresses of morality weighing on our shoulders,

Yet, find peace through it all

Because once we depart this earth

It will be all we have left.

TWENTY-FOUR

We all have the same 24

The same morning, noon, & night

Which all happen after sunrise.

The same 24 to push forward,

Or get pulled back,

The same 24 to mature,

And never look back.

Time is of the essence; we lose every second

To be alive & grow old is only a blessing.

MESSAGE

Some things are better left unsaid,

Better left unread,

Because words hold weight,

They weigh us down.

The adage says something about sticks and stones,

Breaking bones,

And words not hurting;

But if they didn't hurt,

We wouldn't be so quick to leave people left on read,

We wouldn't be so quick to ignore,

Or not communicate, and leave things left unsaid.

PERSPECTIVE

You can't please everyone

And you can't make everyone happy.

We've been conditioned to conform to social norms and when we deviate from regular,

Opinions form.

But if I listen to you,

You,

AND you,

Where's room for myself?

PRESSURE (DOESN'T) BREAK PIPES

Don't let the pressure build to the point you break,

Instead,

Let it be a testament to your strength.

JULY

Changed:
Meaning I am no longer the same,
And neither are you.
As time passes,
Some become wiser,
Others become complacent.
Some work harder,
Others become content.
But time keeps passing,
The sun rises and sets
One day flows into the next,
And we all get older.

What changes will you make,
Or do you wish to remain the same?

RESILIENCE

He felt like he needed redemption

Often overlooked

Often misunderstood

Often underrated

But he knew his own potential

And that made all the difference.

FAR FROM FINISHED

Take a step back
And look how far you've come
Look how far He's brought you,
And God is still not done.

FOUNDATION

We live in the past,
Chasing after what once was
Chasing after what we remember
Chasing after memories.

Looking through old pictures
Of friends
Of family
Of lost loved ones,
Just to feel something.

We've gotten lost,
In the everyday bustle of life
Forgetting where we come from,
But not where we're headed
Our eyes always on the prize,
But we forget our glasses;

We are blinded,
Not by the light
But by the attempt to forget our past
To forget our pain
To forget our foundation––

Which ultimately erases a part of who we are,

And breaks down the very same foundation that took a lifetime to build from the ground up.

daffodils

rebirth, new beginnings

CURRENT

We rise then we fall, again.

This is love

This is life

It's the human current;

Like brainwaves

Or a heartbeat

We open and we close,

Empty and fill,

Waiting for that special one so that

We may rise, but never have to fall again.

NEW BEGINNINGS

This new life

That I created

Began when you left

Because you weren't my happily ever after.

(Constant) Fear

He was scared.

Scared of everything ahead of him,

Of what the future beheld

Feelings intensifying by the day,

He felt stuck, cemented

Unable to express

Unable to communicate because of past trauma

So he removed himself,

And to this day, he's still scared to fall in love.

WHAT IS LOVE

Operating from the heart space always left her so
vulnerable

She opened up to those she experienced,

Giving pieces of herself away,

She wasn't whole.

She felt everything and was "too emotional."

Once she started taking her clothes off it was easier,

But is this what love is?

REDEMPTION

Pick yourself up

And put the pieces back together.

Rebuild your brokenness,

And become better than you were before.

The road is not easy,

The journey will be challenging,

But wouldn't you prefer to get up instead of lying there defeated?

MIRROR IMAGE

When you look within,

And realize that you are your only competition,

You can elevate to the next level.

We hold ourselves back;

We convince ourselves that it's someone else,

Better yet, *something* else.

But,

If you shift your mindset,

And look in the mirror,

You're already halfway there.

ZERO EXPECTATIONS

In this lifetime,

Expect nothing.

It can be taken or given

Flipped and switched

Someone can up and leave,

All in an instant;

And there you are stuck

Not knowing to move up, down, left, or right

But hold yourself to the notion

That if you expect nothing to be given,

You'll be the winner in the end.

MAZIE

Awakened from the ground up

Nurtured in her arms

She's been by my side since day one.

Instilling lifelong lessons and values one by one,

Never resting because a mother's work is never done.

But today all I want,

Is to thank her for everything,

To let her know that she's always appreciated,

Sent straight from heaven,

Mothers are the biggest blessings.

SENIOR

Thank you for teaching me the ropes.

For showing me the way of life

How to navigate,

And how everything goes.

Many lessons learned

A lot of wisdom to discern,

Forever grateful,

Always thankful,

To have someone like you to look up to.

orchids

refinement, growth, maturity

BITTERSWEET

Tucked away, off the grid

Riding through the desert with the top off,

Smiling at each other in the cotton-candy skies;

If we could pause time

And cherish this moment

Like nothing else exists,

Our love would persist;

But the seconds keep ticking

And time keeps moving on.

BONNIE AND CLYDE

If we could backtrack and retrace our steps

To when we first met,

I wouldn't change a thing.

We started placing one brick on top of another,

Building our home,

Building our trust

I was getting to know you.

Building our future, building us.

But things didn't pan out, we didn't have favor on our side

We could've been a modern-day Bonnie and Clyde.

LOST

You weren't ready
But I didn't know it
So you left
So you could find yourself
Then find me again.

RATIO

If you could meet me halfway,

We could make this more than a summertime fling

You could be my thing,

Me and you: us.

But you were never good at math,

And 80/20 is not half.

DANGER

If this world were ours,

I would be the water that nourishes you every day,

You would be the seeds beneath the soil

And we could grow together.

Halves of each other that make one, we would reflect.

Soul ties, beyond the superficial

Ties for eternity;

Though we just met, I'm already down for the journey

Your piercing eyes and white smile lead me into the
darkness,

You're dangerous.

SEVEN

My past trauma

Is guarding the door

And isn't allowing you to enter.

As much as I want to open the door

And let you in,

My baggage blocks the doorway,

Tripping you as you run towards me,

But I can't help you

I can't help 'it'

It's a part of me.

I'm learning to unpack my bags and only take what I need

But thank you for understanding,

Thank you for bearing with me.

NOT ENOUGH SPACE

I could only wish,

That both of our worlds could exist,

That we could coexist,

And everything be bliss.

Yet there's three of us,

But only room for two.

TIME AWAY

This feeling is new.
"Is time away necessary?"
"Is time away needed?"
Are questions that run through my head as I try to
decipher my new reality.

I don't want to say I lost you because you're still here,
And I don't want to say it's over because of my internal
fear;
Time away makes me miss you more,
But will too much time away have the same effect?
If I get myself together and reset,
Will you get to the point where you neglect?

If we both had all of the answers
Neither of us would be in this position
If I had all of the answers
I wouldn't have presented this situation;

There's no happy ending
Because we're in limbo,
Time will only tell where our relations will go.

RUNNING THROUGH MY VEINS

Trying to process your pain, as if it's mine,

It hurts.

From the outside, I never viewed you as broken--

And not that you are,

But you keep it together well.

In your eyes I see the pain,

Your voice crackles, nothing is the same

My love for you runs so deep in my veins,

I can't help but shed a tear too

All these years and all you've been through,

I would have never known that you needed tending to.

But thank you for sharing, for even letting me in

Taking me back to day one where it all began

To understand you is to understand myself

I'm your shoulder to lean on,

Through sickness and health.

HEALING

Years after the fact,
The pain still hurts the same.

The wound may be closed, but the stitches are still there
She may have moved on, but she still checks for him in
her rearview;

She sees that he's happy now and she's still getting to that
point,
She has to keep pushing forward to reach her peace of
mind and her own clear view.

PERFECTLY IMPERFECT

She painted a picture as if she had it all together
Yet piercing beneath her layers, I could see deeper within;
Her jaded smile not enough to hide years of brokenness,
She put on a front,
Because she didn't want me to know she's flawed.
But that's the beauty of it all,
I didn't expect her to be perfect.

LION

I have too much pride,

With time on my side,

To run back to where we once were.

Done being the good guy,

In you I can no longer confide,

I won't run back to where we once were.

But if you find yourself,

Then come back to me,

Maybe we can meet in the middle.

SESSION 33

If I opened my eyes and woke up to you every morning,

I would be satisfied.

My prayers answered,

My dreams fulfilled,

Our kids would be able to experience how true love feels;

A bigger love that encompasses all,

A love that leaves us in awe,

But you're out of sight

Yet I don't know if you'll ever leave my mind.

BUTTERFLIES

When you flutter across my mind,

I get butterflies.

When I think of our time together,

I can't help but wonder,

Why you're stuck in my mind,

And not right here by my side.

A YEAR WASTED

I wonder if I would've been better off not knowing you existed;

Then I wouldn't be yearning for more, there would be nothing to be missing

I wouldn't be going back and forth with myself wondering if you feel for me

Wondering if I cross your mind and if you want to be mine

Neither of us would be in this predicament

There would be no time wasted

But here we are

Ten months in

Feeling like we just began,

And I don't know how much more time I can spend

Wondering, hoping, and just praying that you feel me.

sweet peas

appreciation and departure

MUTUAL FEELINGS

We were once united:
Coffee and creamer mixed in the morning,
Individual raindrops that combined to form a stream
streaking down the window,
We were miniature rocks forming sand on the beach;
I would pick you up from the train station after your long
days at work
I would have dinner at home waiting, wine on the table,
The kids couldn't wait to see you.

Though you're still their mother:
Work wasn't work,
Your coworker was more than a coworker,
And you were tired from something else.
No longer one,
Only coffee, no creamer,
An individual raindrop
A singular grain of sand,

Mutual Feelings.

NAMELESS

The sun sets

The moon rises

And you are still on my mind.

Tides come and tides go

Yet I can't leave you behind.

No matter how much I try,

I cannot resist

For you were my soulmate

And are deeply missed.

I have to move on,

For my own sanity

I can't allow one person

To have this much control over me

Three breaths in

And three breaths out

I've cleared my brain of you

Until you return again tomorrow

Texting my phone, doing that thing that you always do.

R.E.M

I woke up excited,

Because you came to me in a dream.

It was like old times,

And I thought you still cared.

I soon realized it was a fantasy.

Me creating a false narrative for you

      That was easily too good to be true.

Back to sleep I go,

Life seems better in my dreams anyway.

I Think I'm in Love

I think I'm in love.

Red petals, green leaves, prickly stems
The smell of spring in the air
The birds flying, the sun shining
A cloudless day, not a worry in the way,
I think I'm in love.

Red hearts, blue texts, funny tweets,
Her scent that I never get tired of
Her voice, her laughter
A genuine person, not a worry in the way,
I think I'm in love.

But it was all a facade–
Never able to admit to your issues,
Left me questioning my character.
Jaded by the superficial,
But now brought back to earth,

I thought I was in love.

EMPTY CANVAS

Still thinking about you and what could have been,
Reminiscing on us and the little time we spent:
Time we spent learning one another,
Time we spent beginning to evolve together.
We were only growing up, toward the sunlight
But our growth was stunted by your past
And your inability to be open,
Yet I was an open canvas for you to paint on.

But you left me blank,
Then you left altogether.

TWO BIRDS

At peace with knowing I gave my all

Like two birds in a tree, we had love at first sight

We looked into the future and saw reflections of
ourselves,

We were naive.

Excited to find someone similar but different,

This type of love was rare,

We didn't want to miss it.

But moving too fast,

We fell head over heels,

And my all became

Nothing.

IT WAS A PHASE

I learned from you, you learned from me

Invested in each other in hopes of blooming together, we were seeds

You were planted by your ex and I planted myself, we were incompatible

On different levels of development, we could never sprout together

But the time we spent in the soil was worthwhile.

It was only a phase.

CASSETTE

I found some of your old clothes at my place

Pieces of you that reminded me of what we once had

You're in my rear view

You're a figment of my past

But now I'm on the verge of leaving all of the heartbreak and hurt behind,

Let's pick up where we left off,

And press rewind.

BETTER WITHOUT YOU

I was naive,

To believe that we could work things out,

That I could right my wrongs,

I was selfish.

Wanted to do what was best for me

Without considering what was best for you,

You always pulled out the best in me.

But now I know:

That we can't always have what we want

And healing is not a two-way street

You need time

You need space

Focus on you, I'll focus on me.

JUST BECAUSE

You trickle across my mind in the wee hours of the night,

Just because.

I don't think I miss you

But in these hours,

I can't live without you.

Memories of us, flood my brain

Our connection, the time we spent, and our dates,

Now it's not the same.

Just because we aren't one,

Doesn't eliminate us being two halves of each other.

Down the road, our souls will match,

And we'll find one another,

Again.

SET ME FREE

How does one keep going,

When I'm held back

Like a dog on a leash,

Or an animal in the zoo,

By all the memories we made?

You won't leave my head,

No matter how much I try to forget.

Yet eventually,

Time will pass,

Memories will fade,

And everything that reminds me of you will be meaningless.

THE GOOD ONES

She didn't question the things I did

She let me be

She didn't look too deep,

She trusted me.

Open communication with no boundaries,

She was the one.

Too bad I missed an opportunity

Because I just wanted some fun,

Because I was interested in someone

Else.

I've learned though that the good ones don't last long in the open

Because it was far too late once I got the notion.

OXYGEN

You told me empty lies that filled my heart like a balloon;
Now I'm deflated, searching for more air.

IVY

We were once one:

Rooted in the same soil, we grew together.

Taking different paths towards the sun,

We met halfway into our lives

Our roots intertwined as we intertwined in our bedsheets,

You were all I knew.

Then you uprooted and got tangled in ivy,

No longer pure.

You ran back to me trying to pot yourself in the same soil,

And I wanted to let you back in,

But poison ivy would only stunt my growth.

EMPTY

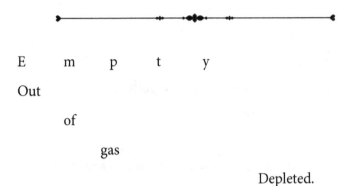

E   m   p   t   y

Out

      of

           gas

                          Depleted.

As if I'm speeding 100 mph down the freeway,

Everything is a blur.

No gas stations in sight,

             No love in sight,

               I did everything in my capacity,

But I can't even get a refill.

AND I STILL

And I still think about you:

Your smile

Your laugh

Your dimples, well dimple, right in the middle of your left
cheek

And I still think about your brown eyes that peered into
mine,

Your brown eyes that were a reflection of me.

I still think about us,

I still think about what we could be,

And I still miss you the way you never missed me.

SEASONAL CHANGES

You served your purpose,

But there's no love lost.

Lessons learned

No bridges burned

My love doesn't come with a cost;

Rather you elevated me

And I uplifted you

You were only around for a season

But the lessons will last a lifetime.

JUNE 22ND

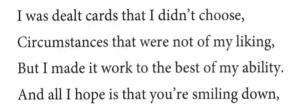

I was dealt cards that I didn't choose,
Circumstances that were not of my liking,
But I made it work to the best of my ability.
And all I hope is that you're smiling down,
Proud of me.

LIFE GOES ON

If I never saw you again,

I'd be okay;

Because I read all of your chapters,

And you read mine.

I experienced you and all you had to offer,

And you could say the same about me.

Sometimes we get bored of reading the same book,

Sometimes love dies;

All in all, you were a good read

But love isn't as simple as it seems.

LOSE IT ALL

I'm holding on to the remaining pieces of me.
I want to make sure I don't lose everything,
In the midst of it all.

My sanity and my foundation
Are two things I must keep
So that I may reap what I sow,
That I may hold on,
And maintain perfect peace,
In the midst of it all.

UNTIL WE MEET AGAIN

Our dreams, wants, hopes, and visions
Are nothing short of our potential
God would not place them in our heads if they were not
achievable;

I took a step out on faith,
Thank you for joining and making my dream believable.

ABOUT THE AUTHOR

Armond Gray Jr. is currently a fourth-year Kinesiology major, Spanish minor at Chapman University. He is also a Provost Scholarship Award Winner and a three-year team captain of the Men's Track and Field Team. During the 2019-2020 school year, he was a Physical Therapy research assistant at Chapman, and during the current 2020-2021 school year, he is a Resident Advisor. In the Fall of 2020, Armond's poem, "The Pain My Ancestors Felt", was featured in Chapman's *The Panther* Publication, and more recently, his poem, "We Didn't Ask to be Here", was featured in Carvd N Stone's *Best of CNS 2020* magazine publication as well. While away from school, Armond enjoys traveling, listening to music, exercising, and photography.

He expects to graduate in May of 2021 from Chapman University with a B.S. in Kinesiology and a Spanish minor. He is from San Francisco, and you can keep up with him @armond.poetry on Instagram.

I would not be here, and none of this
would have been possible without either
of my parents: my Mother, Antoinette
Crawley-Acoff, and my Father, Armond
Gray Sr. Thank you again for always
believing in me and for giving me life!

Cheers to both of you! ♡

CPSIA information can be obtained
at www.ICGtesting.com
Printed in the USA
FSHW020015290321
79899FS